African American Inventors and their Inventions A-Z

Written by Anita C. President, Ed.D
Illustrated by Karen Clopton-Dunson

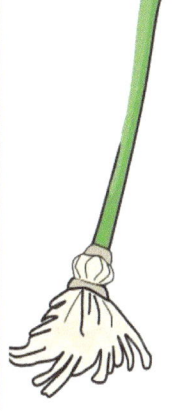

Copyright © 2017 by Anita C. President, Ed.D
All rights reserved. No part of this publication may be reproduced, distributed, or transmitted in any form or by any means, including photocopying, recording, or other electronic or mechanical methods, without the prior written permission of the publisher, except in the case of brief quotations embodied in critical reviews and certain other noncommercial uses permitted by copyright law.

Thank You

A special thanks to my mother and father, Alberta and Robert Curtis, who stressed the importance of education. My daughter, Alexandria for her cheer-leading spirit and support. My family :David, Eugene, Gerald, Louise, and Toni for their encouragement. Also, Calumet High School for introducing an African American History Class into the curriculum (after the Chicago Teachers Union fought and won this during contract negotiations).

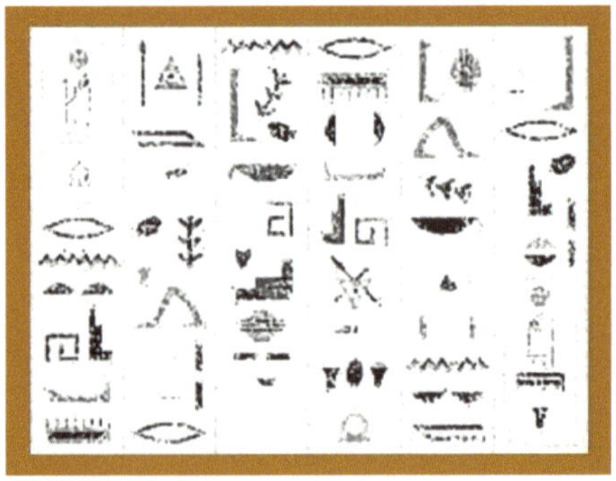

 is for alphabet

The Africans in Egypt gave us the alphabet.
Learning to read and write is the best thing yet.

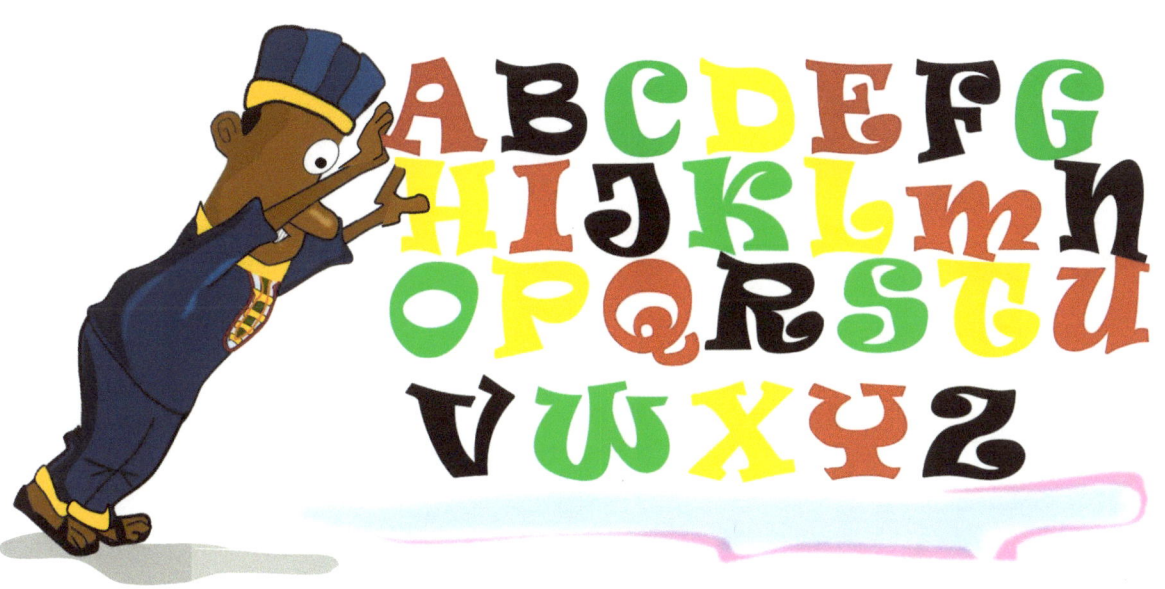

B Is for brush

Where would we be without the brush for our hair?
Lydia Newman wants us to use it with flair.

C is for Clock

Tick-Tock, Tick-Tock,

Benjamin Banneker invented the clock.

D is for dust pan

Lloyd Ray invented the dust pan.
Keeping things clean was his plan.

E is for elevator

The elevator moves from the top floor to the ground.
Thanks to Alexander Miles, it is easier to get around.

F is for fire extinguisher

Fire extinguishers are designed to put fires out. Thomas Martin shows this helps without a doubt.

G is for gas mask

Garrett A. Morgan invented the gas mask.
Saving lives was a dangerous task.

 is for horse shoe

> Horse shoes is a game you can play.
> Oscar Brown designed it that way.
> He, also, designed it for the hoof of a horse.
> We can't forget that, of course.

I is for ironing board

The ironing board was invented by Sarah Boone.

Now you can press your clothes while singing a tune.

J is for Julian's eye medicine

Percy Julian invented a potion for your sight.
It helps you see things clear and bright.

K is for kitchen table

Henry A. Jackson invented the kitchen table.
Come eat with your family whenever you're able.

L is for lawnmower

John Albert Burr invented the lawn mower.
Grass always looks better when it is lower.

M is for mop

Thomas W. Stewart invented the mop,
to keep floors clean in your house or shop.

N is for nursery chair

Lula O. Carter invented the portable nursery chair. Now, you can potty train your baby anywhere.

O is for Ozzie's Williams rocket engine

A small rocket engine was Ozzie's invention.
Helping Apollo land on the moon was his intention.

P is for pencil sharpener

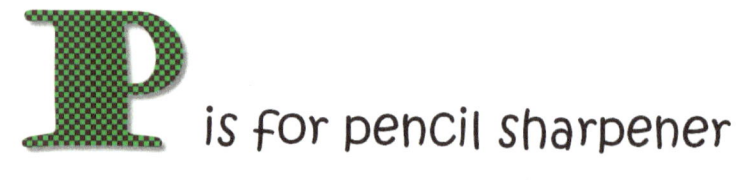

John L. Love invented a sharpener for your pencil.
He hoped it would be your favorite writing utensil.

Q is for quilting frame

Thomas Elkins invented the quilting frame.
Making quilts easier to do is his claim to fame.

R is for roller coaster

Granville T. Woods invented the roller coaster.
"I can ride with my hands up," cried the boaster.

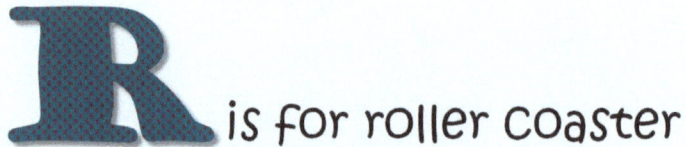

S is for super soaker

Lonnie G. Johnson invented the super soaker.
If you make me wet, I'll call you a joker.

T is for tricycle

If you've ridden on one, I'm sure you had tons of fun. Matthew A. Cherry's invention of the early tricycle is second to none.

U is for umbrella stand

William C. Carter made the umbrella stand.
So that when you're in the house, you won't hold it in your hand.

V is vacuum pan

Norbert Rillieux invented the vacuum pan.
This is how processing sugar all began.

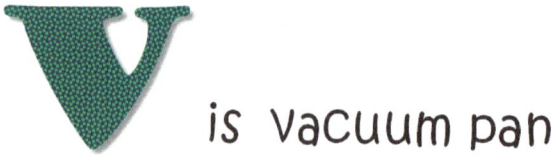

 is for water sprinkler

Joseph A. Smith invented the sprinkler for your hose.
Keeping your grass healthy and green is the reason, I suppose.

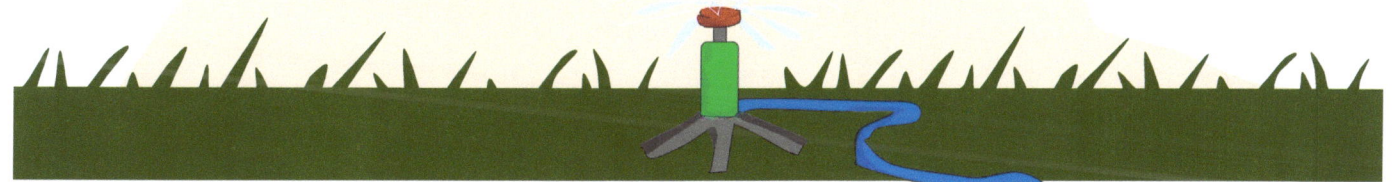

 is for x-ray machine

A portable x-ray machine Frederick Jones did make.
Pictures of your insides are now easier for doctors to take.

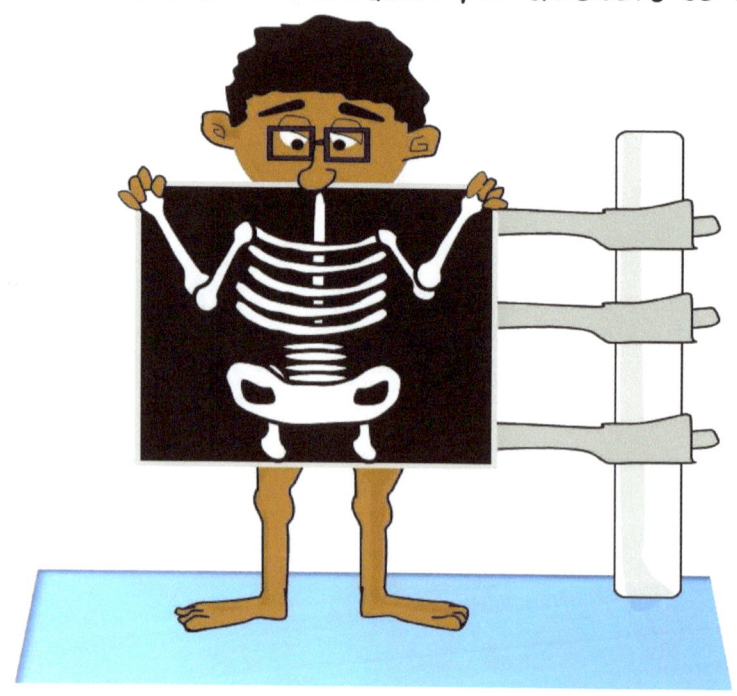

Y is for yarn holder

Julia Hammond invented the yarn holder.
No more yarn wrapped around your shoulder.

Z is for zirconia processing

The zirconia gemstone is shiny and bright. Thanks to Johnathan Smith, they sparkle in the morning, noon, or night.

Anita Curtis-President has been a Head Teacher and Parent Resource Teacher in the Child-Parent Centers of Chicago. She has also, taught kindergarten and first grade in the Chicago Public Schools, She holds the following degrees: BA in Education, MA in Educational Leadership, Doctorate in Education. She has always found time to educate the children and their parents about the contributions of African Americans. The author has one daughter, Alexandria ,and they live in Chicago. This is her first children's book.

Invention	Inventor	Date of Invention	Patent Number
Alphabet	Egyptians	N/A	N/A
Brush	Lydia Newman	November 15, 1898	614,335
Clock	Benjamin Banneker	1753	N/A
Dust Pan	Lloyd Ray	August 3, 1897	587,335
Elevator	Alexander Miles	October 11, 1887	371,207
Fire Extinguisher	Thomas J. Martin	March 26, 1872	125,063
Gas Mask	Garrett Morgan	October 13, 1914	1,113,675
Horseshoe	Oscar Brown	August 23, 1892	461,271
Ironing Board	Sarah Boone	April 26, 1892	473,653
Glaucoma Drug	Percy Julian	1935	
Kitchen Table	Henry A. Jackson	October 6, 1896	596,135
Lawn Mower	John Albert Burr	May 9, 1899	624,749
Mop	Thomas W. Stewart	June 13, 1893	499,402
Nursery Chair	Lula O. Carter	February, 9, 1960	2,923,950
Small Rocket Engine	Ozzie Williams	1961	
Pencil Sharpener	John L. Love	November 23, 1897	594,114
Quilting Frame	Thomas Elkins	February 22, 1870	100,020
Roller Coaster	Granville T. Woods	December 19, 1899	639,692
Super Soaker	Lonnie O. Johnson	September 29, 1992	5,150,819
Tricycle (Velocipede)	Matthew A. Cherry	May 8, 1888	382,351
Umbrella Stand	William C. Carter	August 4, 1885	323,397
Vaccuum Pan	Norbert Rillieux	August 26, 1843	3,237
Water Sprinkler	Joseph A. Smith	May 4, 1897	581,785
X-ray Machine (portable)	Frederick M. Jones	1920's	Did not apply for one
Yarn Holder	Julia Hammond	December 15, 1896	572,985
Zirconia composition process	Johnathan Smith	March 11, 1969	3,432,314

CPSIA information can be obtained
at www.ICGtesting.com
Printed in the USA
LVHW072116270122
709582LV00002B/99